SHARDS

RESTORING THE SHATTERED SPIRIT

WALTER COOPER

Illustrated by the author

Health Communications, Inc.
Deerfield Beach, Florida

Library of Congress Cataloging-in-Publication Data

Cooper, Walter
  Shards: restoring the shattered spirit / Walter Cooper; illustrated by the author.
      p.   cm.
  Includes bibliographical references.
  ISBN 1-55874-246-8
  1. Cooper, Walter, 1939 —   2. Religious biography — United States.   3. Spiritual life.   I. Title.
BL73.C66A3   1992   92-18757
291.4—dc20   CIP

©1992 Walter Cooper
ISBN 1-55874-246-8

All rights reserved. Printed in the United States of America. No part of this publication may be reproduced, stored in a retrieval system or transmitted in any form or by any means, electronic, mechanical, photocopying, recording or otherwise without the written permission of the publisher.

Publisher: Health Communications, Inc.
           3201 S.W. 15th Street
           Deerfield Beach, Florida 33442-8190

Cover art: Walter Cooper
Cover design: Iris T. Slones and Walter Cooper

For Billy, Bob, Brian, Chris,
Darrell, Don, Frank, Gary, Graham,
Hallie, Jay, Joe, Larry, Laughlin, Lynn,
Michael, Peter, Phil, Rick, Rodrick, Ron, Russell,
Thomas, Tim, Trinity, Tuck, William and the legions
of others who suffer or have suffered from AIDS,
I dedicate these pages. Brave young lions who
dare to cross the thrashing river are first
to rest on the silent shore.

When sorrows come, they come not single spies,
But in battalions.

Hamlet

CONTENTS

Introduction	ix
1. Strike An Unmarked Trail	1
2. Gifts Of The Great Spirit	41
3. Conversations With Raven	81
4. Tapping Into The Magical	121
5. Near To The Primal Heart	161
6. Hunting The Inheritance	201
Acknowledgments	241
Chapter Notes	243

INTRODUCTION

For two thousand years the Pueblo people made simple clay bowls. Unique vessels shaped with skill by prehistoric craftsmen of the American Southwest. Bowls made spherical and smooth to touch, bowls of radiant beauty.

Using a yucca brush, women artists would carefully decorate their handiwork with a dazzling array of graphic designs representing the forces of their natural world — lightning, water, clouds, mountains, wild animals. Bowls were painted with leaping antelopes and playful rabbits, pesky bugs and elusive quail. Serpents, snakes, fish and men were frequent motifs.

Pottery was an integral and enduring part of Pueblo life — a living spirit which always served a functional role. It held the food to nourish exhausted hunters. It carried the water to douse a desert thirst. Large storage jars held corn, beans and pine nuts to sustain clans throughout the long frigid winters. It held the seeds for spring.

Bowls were widely used in the great ritual ceremonies and held sacred offerings to the immortal spirit.

When the time came to pass on to another world, a large handsomely painted bowl was sometimes placed over the head of the deceased, and together, bowl and man were returned to their Mother Clay who gave them birth.

Today in New Mexico where I live, there are innumerable remnants of times gone by. Abandoned for centuries, crumbling Anasazi and Mogollon villages, or *pueblos* as they were called by the invading Spanish, punctuate the arid landscape. Several of these mud-walled or sandstone ruins which I like to explore are hidden away in the vast Galisteo Basin.

Very little remains at most of these sites, however, except mounds of earth covered with cholla cactus and chamisa, nothing to signify the ancient activity that once flourished here. Nothing, that is, but countless small pieces of broken pottery, or shards, which litter virtually every site.

Why do they fascinate me so, these curious tokens of the past? Is it because I, too, need to establish a *spirit line,* a meaningful connection with something primeval, organic and whole? Again and again I am drawn to these random bits of clay as if they were clues to the source of my own well-being.

I pick up a few shards and examine them. Running my finger slowly across their broken edges and curved lip, I notice a fragment of a design and wonder what the rest of the pattern might be. Not wishing to disturb the site, I usually put the shards back on the ground where I found them. But not always.

Walter Cooper

1

STRIKE AN UNMARKED TRAIL

*Let us see, is this real,
This life I am living?*

Pawnee

I am never fulfilled, numb from trying. I'm tired of bottom-fishing, of getting hopelessly snagged on the narrow spaces of my illusions. Why not reel me in — toss me back in the bucket of squirming crawlers — and bait the hook with more promising fare?

Remembered clips of dreams remind me that I am capable of better painting, better writing, more abundant and zestful living than my worldly state of affairs suggests. I wish I were a soda jerk with soda jerk ambitions. I wish I were a kinder, less critical person who harbored no resentment.

It's the unrealized hungers of ours which lead us to cling to people and to things and to the beliefs of our human condition. If we search for our essential food any place other than the source, we search in vain. So we slumber on fitfully, waiting for the magic kiss which never comes.

Lives in rapid transit. Never in human history have so many changes pelted us as they do today. Startling new information storms us from all directions. Whatever our work is about, it has the life span of a gnat. Whatever our life's about, it all gets lost in the latest dance step. Now, more than ever, we need something enduring to hold close, something that won't wash away in the furious tides of change.

How quickly we get tangled in the web of our busy schedules. Too many activities, overwhelming commitments, endless maintenance chores and obligations. Soon we are tied up in knots, weary and defeated by a world relentlessly pulling us apart.

We know that life is too precious to waste on the expectations of others, too fleeting to squander on hollow goals. But how do we save ourselves from those squadrons of "shoulds" which steal our creative fire and rekindle the heart's natural blaze?

If we examine each of our "sacred cows," we might just see how many "shoulds" it takes to keep them all in clover.

Why are we always trying to make better, to improve? Why are we possessed with ever-nagging doubts about not being appreciated enough, or successful enough, or healthy enough, or attractive enough, never quite measuring up? Never satisfied. Never enough.

I need a long vacation. A sabbatical away from myself. I need to let go, to relax in this futile struggle against myself. To examine my thoughts and to realize the synthetic nature of my fears. To wonder why I am here in this world.

Silver concha belts and turquoise finger rings are no substitute for the delight that's missing in our hearts.

The human condition is a tired old bus crammed full of humanity. We have broken down completely on a rickety bridge over a black abyss. Under our immense weight, the aged span is beginning to give. What are we to do? Try to fix a decrepit bus or abandon it immediately and get off the bridge pronto?

Trying to patch the world's vast problems is like trying to hold water in a leaky radiator. We waste valuable time and limited resources. Solutions to our worldly concerns lie in our inner transformation, not outward repair.

By the term *human condition* I mean all that has been fabricated by the fertile mind of humankind, the sum total of all our collective imagination: all of our myths and histories, our myriad cultures and religions, our staggering inventory of fears and beliefs — all that the human brain has invented.

There is much to admire in mankind's resumé but if we are to embark on an outing of conscience, our first obligation is to see more clearly. To recognize those corrupt systems which threaten life on earth and to begin to distinguish what is real from what is not.

Out of this human condition also comes the ignorance which is responsible for all fear, hate, war, poverty, shame, the widespread brutishness of life on earth.

Only by breaking away and freeing myself from the prevailing belief systems which created these conditions initially, do I have a chance for spiritual growth.

It hit me like a flash flood, this cleansing idea that God cannot exist in our human condition. Human conditions are temporary, like stage sets. Worldly, earthbound and transitory because they mirror attitudes and beliefs popular at any given period in world history but certain to shift or collapse with time and circumstance.

How can I find God among man's flimsy concepts and constructions? He is not there. They are not of his making.

God's bright angels are hiding from most of us, so we will have to set a trap for them. If they do not exist in the human condition as suggested, then where do they exist? Or do they exist at all?

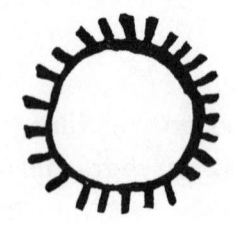

Since the aborigine first opened his eyes, mankind has fueled and maintained mighty beliefs regarding birth and death. Birth is seen as the genesis of life, the auspicious beginning; whereas death is viewed as the final curtain, the terrifying end.

But what if both concepts are deceptive? What if we've been tricked by our sensory perception and there is no truth to the appearance of birth or death? What if what we're seeing are but vivid visual effects which radically alter the appearance of matter, and we have been mesmerized or moved or spooked by these effects?

Our identifying system is one more faulty invention of *Homo sapiens* which leads to great confusion and pain. From the nursery on, we are taught to regard ourselves strictly as *Man* or as *Woman*. As Black or as White. As Christian or Jew. Liberal or Conservative. Old or young. Saint or sinner. Gay or straight. Have or have-not. In or out, pro or con, this or that.

Why must our lives be an either-or situation? We needn't categorize ourselves or anybody else according to appearances or superficial condition. We are all of the above. We are none of the above. We are, that's all.

If He's up there, would you ask Him to answer the phone. Things down here are a hopeless jumble. We look to heaven for justice and understanding but seldom receive any satisfactory answers. So we turn to other more available gods who seem to dwell within our grasp and tantalize with quick fixes and easy solutions.

What I'm getting at is this. We've bought it and we're paying for it (it isn't cheap). We take it home and set it up, plug it in and stand back, take a good look and find it strangely wanting. Maybe another color, another model, another brand? Can we take it back and try again? What if . . .?

Somewhere along the road well-trampled I began to suspect that the accepted reality to which I had unconsciously subscribed had little to do with growing a soul. Led by curiosity, I began to notice others who saw their world differently and I was drawn in by their words and unorthodox ideas. Buckminster Fuller was one of the first. His books were followed by those of other august thinkers: Carlos Castaneda, Nikos Kazantzakis, Hermann Hesse, C. S. Lewis, Edward Abbey. What boat-rockers! One book led to another, one author to another. Lyall Watson to Joel Goldsmith. M.C. Richards to Elisabeth Kübler-Ross. Maria Montessori to Alice Miller. Ken Carey to Krishnamurti.

Like innocent young calves we are rounded up and branded with white hot beliefs identifying our particular cultural heritage or ethnic mix. Our entire school experience is an exercise in measurement and competition, forever graded and compared. Finally, after a desultory education of outrageous initiation, we are prodded and pushed into the world arena with all the repressed anger and hostility of raging bulls.

Appearances, style, manners, background, education — they all speak volumes about our human identity, but they have little to do with the *élan vital,* that creative dragon which stirs within.

Growing up in the '50s, in the frosty Republican atmosphere of cautious conservatism and conformity, was much more dangerous than anyone realized. The casualty count among my peers attests to this. The genteel folks who raised us were generally caring and well-meaning, but our souls and senses were gravely underfed.

All the mothers I knew were unfulfilled and nervous. Dads seemed uniformly industrious and emotionally unavailable to their children. Our tight, white, upper-middle-class suburban world was discreetly awash in alcohol. Breaking away from the paralyzing sense of incapacity and fear, which these conditions ultimately foster, has become the major struggle of my life.

Often those who hurt us most in life unwittingly give us the most valuable gift. They provide the jolt which initiates a spark which produces the change that was long overdue.

Occasionally a soothing air would pass by the stifled rooms of childhood hinting of a *spirit line* which courses throughout all creation.

"I'm up to *here* in work," sighs Dung Beetle. "It clutters up my house and mind. Out of here with all that stuff! I want to simplify and travel light."

In the upstairs hallway of my mind there is a door marked "Impossible." I want to yank that portal off its hinges.

The year 1973 was my turning point. No longer could I live the life, real or imagined, that others expected of me. I had to find out who I was and what potentials were concealed in me. I needed to listen to my own smothered voice whatever its song might be.

Farewell, New York, I headed West in my VW bug. Zipping across Illinois, Iowa, Nebraska, I began to grapple with my new found freedom. John Denver was singing on the radio about coming home to a place he'd never been before, just as the Rocky Mountains spread out before me. The words struck home. It was the summer of my thirty-third year, and I was starting over again after my promising career in advertising fizzled in failure and firing. With no idea of what lay ahead or what to do next, I headed South on I-25 at the Colorado border, a muddle of despair.

When we find ourselves at the wrong clambake, we can always split. Exit. Just get up and go find ourselves more suitable accommodations. That's what founded America! Do whatever you have to do to claim your own life. Leaving bleak, unhappy circumstances behind is always an option and often the best choice.

"We are more the products of our choices than we are the victims of our circumstances," added Armadillo who recently moved to Amarillo.

My desolate state disarmed me at once. The kiln-dry desert with its unexpected openness and unrestricted views. Terra-cotta mesas speckled with piñon trees. Limitless plains dotted with mauve mountains. Yellow oxide cliffs. Cerulean blue skies. Flat matte colors empowered with incandescent light. New Mexico. Painters' country! I was galvanized.

Soon I found the companionship of other pilgrims who had also left their roots behind to move to an unknown place where lives could be lived differently. Those who valued their personal liberty above all. I found the strength of native people and the blessed solitude of the silent drifting hawk.

The minute I arrived, I knew I was hooked. (Breath quickens and blood pounds at 7,000 feet above sea level.) My brain reeled as it does sometimes when I hit on something I was craving. My other self — my intuitive self — had steered me to the place it had been searching for.

Just in time, my heart's on empty, my spirit's reached a record low. I'm scattered and lost, a dried up potshard left on this timeless land waiting for something wondrous to happen.

Then, suddenly, a claret cup cactus blooms . . .

She had recently moved to Santa Fe from Tucson when we first met. Years before, she had been a student/instructor at Black Mountain College in North Carolina where she studied with a renowned collection of radical thinkers from the world of contemporary art and design. She met Bucky Fuller at Black Mountain. Once they constructed an early model of a geodesic dome from Venetian blind slats they'd found in the attic.

Confined to a wheelchair due to childhood polio, she sat proud and confident in her rented house on Canyon Road. She planned to start a school for young children in Santa Fe as she had done in Arizona. In the meantime, she would put together groups of artists and others committed to self-discovery. Her soft full body and her bright pink face were crowned by a nimbus of fleecy white hair. Hugging Hazel, a friend remarked, was like hugging a cloud.

She asked me what I thought the word "spiritual" meant, and I said something flippant about contact with my dead grandmother, or making tables rise in midair. She smiled patiently, then said, "The spiritual movement is really a perceptual movement. Any unfoldment in perception is an unfoldment of the spirit."

I wanted to know more, so I enrolled in her ongoing weekly class entitled, "A Perceptual Investigation, Or Things Are Not What They Appear To Be." Her fascinating classes and symposiums challenged me, and I continued to go exploring with Hazel for nine years. Looking back on it, I realize that this gentle revolutionary was just the catalyst I needed. She entered my life at an optimum moment. And things have never been the same.

We have been led to believe in the "eternal carrot," as Hazel calls it, the constant state of becoming, the endless enticement in time. We think if we can just keep on "improving" things, that one day we will finally arrive, but that day never comes. We never achieve any periods of real fulfillment because we are never fully connected in the present moment.

"I don't deny the possibility of reincarnation," she says, "but karma and reincarnation are the greatest excuses for non-living. If we always have another life, another chance, maybe *then* we'll get our carrot. Why can't we accept ourselves just as we are? Why must there always be measurement? Don't you see that all the 'shoulds' prevent us from being where we are? It is only in the *now* that anything can happen."

Hazel introduced me to the concept that all spiritual phenomena is "invisible activity." Entertaining this reality can be a riveting exercise. If I am unable to accept things I cannot touch or see, then I am a prisoner of the appearance world.

My eyes can easily be deceived by a desert mirage or a slick magic act. As awareness grows, I see how continually fooled we are by our own five-sense perception. What appears to be our tangible, visible, material world in which we place our trust and sink our tap roots, may indeed be one gigantic illusion or magic spell or *maya,* as the Hindus maintain.

"I've been hornswoggled enough, thank you," said Lemming. "I'm leery of any more misinformation regarding 'my spiritual path.' "

"Quite right!" nodded Red Fox, "but if the real thing came along and bit you on the snout, would you recognize it?"

"Good question," said Lemming.

For many people, the music has faded and the creative spirit is absent from their lives. Religious beliefs and rigid social behavior have straight-jacketed generations with solemn and fearful legacies as well. Countless souls have been woefully misled as to the true nature of their being. We are creatures of sunlight, not sin. Lives needn't be guilty or cheerless or gray. Our natural state is joy!

I'm no writer, I'm a Pack Rat. A scavenger collecting bits and pieces from the rubble of other landscapes. An information-gatherer salvaging particles from our dimly remembered childhood. I would like to offer you the leanest remnants of another possibility. I would like to write one sentence which makes sense to a world in pain. After all, who knows more about pain than the wounded, the lonely and the broken-hearted? In these departments my credentials are impeccable.

We drag around a boxcar of beliefs. A belief in good, a belief in bad. A belief in God — or a disbelief in God. As concoctions of the mind, some beliefs have taken eons to perfect. We shuffle through them like a deck of cards, discarding some, holding tight to others, passing them on to our children.

Then one day, unexpectedly, we stumble onto something. Say we're lost in an activity we love doing when all of a sudden something happens — we catch a glimpse of universal order or uncover a fragment of the master plan. But this has nothing to do with our beliefs. This is unlike anything we've known before.

At first we're taken by surprise, then awed, then excited. Intuitively we know that what we are experiencing is comprehensive in design and that we are an integral part of it! There is something of the miraculous in this, a touch of the divine.

Christ told us, "My kingdom is not of this world," meaning that God's house is on a different street from our human condition; that a separate reality exists for all who seek it here on Earth. Just as it was true twenty centuries ago, it remains true today. Like Christ himself, these sacred planes are ever-present. It is our stubborn and steadfast allegiance to human conditioning which is blocking our innate capacity to soar.

2

GIFTS OF THE GREAT SPIRIT

*Now among the alien gods
with weapons of magic am I*
                    Navajo

Throughout the diverse lands there is one Great Spirit from which all creatures draw their breath. Different tribes have different names for it. Some call it *Father* or *God*. Others call it *Mother* or *Goddess*. It really doesn't matter what we call it or what gender we attribute to it, for it incorporates all there is.

Somewhere down life's winding road, we might come to accept the popular notion that we have little or nothing to offer. Nothing can be further from the truth. The Principle of Supply: I am, therefore I have, applies to all. God's serenity and bounty belong to each of us without exception despite persistent doubts and rumors that somehow we were overlooked.

Every minute of every day we are being bombarded with the most extraordinary offerings. Too bad for us, our receiver sets are turned off. We do not recognize what is naturally ours.

Imagine you're a giant satellite dish able to pick up abundant grace or a super magnet able to draw to you whatever you need to complete your growth. Imagine being a fielder's mitt able to catch the creative impulse. Imagine being the recipient of unconditional love.

Holding title to spiritual gifts does not automatically make them ours. The choice, however, always is — either we can learn to trust in this invisible activity and enter the great mystery or we perpetuate the coma.

We diminish ourselves every time we place our faith outside of ourselves and help to create a society of "authorities." Like Dorothy and her friends in *The Wizard of Oz*, we journey to Emerald City seeking advice from the great and powerful Oz, only to find our wonderful wizard a windy fake. We had the power all along.

If for any reason you are a Lone Wolf and separate or different from the rest of the pack, celebrate! You've been issued a special permit to make important discoveries. Your distance allows you a unique vantage point in a conforming world. You may be able to see what others cannot. Your condition allows you opportunities out of the mainstream of everyday human experience. Recognize the gift and run with it.

Had it not been for my humiliating and frequently painful lack of success on life's gridirons and midways, I doubt my spiritual wake-up call would have been noticed at all.

One troubled night I could not find sleep. My mind pounced on one worry after another faster than a hen on a June bug. It seemed everything I wanted in my life was lacking. Around four in the morning, I popped out of bed, grabbed a pen and quickly jotted something down, then stumbled back to bed. Surprise followed the next morning when I discovered what was written on the paper: "What I need is given to me."

My father showed me the joy that comes from working with your hands. Our happiest times together were spent in his basement shop making picture frames. He taught me how to use tools and patiently explained which tool to use for a certain task. He showed me the deep satisfaction that comes when you love the work that you do.

Mother's influences were much less tangible. She always felt constricted by her financial circumstances and encouraged me to get out in the world and experience life more fully than she had been able to do. Fortifying me with unfailing love, she taught me the value of loyalty and forgiveness.

My parents died a few years ago, but parents are never far away. Our difficulties were substantial and there was dysfunction but never malice. Growing pains and resentments fade with time. I'd give anything for just an hour with them — to see their faces, hear their voices.

Whenever I try to hide from the truth, I am miserable. Truth is a trail that leads to blossoming, to love and ultimately to God. Truth is something we recognize immediately deep in our bones whenever we encounter it. It thrills us clear down to the marrow.

Why do we have such difficulty living in the
present? The past is a vacant seashell. The future is
a mirage pasted together with hope and expectation.
Now is really all there is. Happiness does not
come from either past or future,
but by capturing the live and trembling moment.

Everything we need exists for us right now as these passages so beautifully express.

"Consider the lilies of the field, how they grow; they toil not, neither do they spin:

"Wherefore, if God so clothe the grass of the field, which today is, and tomorrow is cast into the oven, *shall he* not much more *clothe* you, O ye of little faith?

"Therefore take no thought, saying, What shall we eat? or, What shall we drink? or, Wherewithal shall we be clothed?

"For your heavenly Father knoweth that ye have need of all these things.

"But seek ye first the kingdom of God, and his righteousness; and all these things shall be added unto you."

Nineteenth-century English economist Thomas Malthus theorized that population tends to increase faster than the means of subsistence, resulting in an inadequate supply of food and other necessary goods.

Our traditional educational systems continue to give credence to the Malthusian theory and the world mind fervently embraces the idea of scarcity — that there is simply not enough to go around. When enough minds believe in something, it manifests itself physically and becomes our reality, fashioning our own reality.

As science and technology continue to boost agricultural production, we realize there is enough food to feed the planet. But as long as a global view of scarcity prevails (along with the greed and insensitivity it generates), we will continue to witness widespread starvation, or bare subsistence for much of the world, and overconsumption for a relative few.

Our table is already set. Our names are written on unopened gifts. We are well provided for — not always in shares equal to our expectations, perhaps, but should we find ourselves lacking in one course, we may well discover extra servings in another.

My New York career was writing copy for the world's largest advertising agency. There was much discussion in our Creative Department about creativity itself — who had it and who didn't and where inspiration comes from.

Who really created the ceiling frescos of the Sistine Chapel? Did Mozart create *Cosi Fan Tutti?* Did C. S. Lewis singly create his enchanted *Narnia* chronicles? Do parents create their children? All appearances suggest they do, but I wonder.

Can anyone aspire to become the instrument through which an act of co-creation occurs? Those who are, are lifted forever above the ordinary limits of human experience and provide a glorious window for us all. But why are some people selected as conduits of divine expression and others apparently not?

Listen to the rhythms of your own heartbeat. Your body is a miraculous vehicle designed especially for you. It doesn't have to be judged or measured in comparison with other bodies or fouled with anything which may sabotage its performance.

My aching back. Endless hours spent walking loops and swimming laps and doing repetitive strengthening and stretching exercises — and still I suffer from low back and neck pain. Sometimes the spasms are so intense that I'm sent to the hospital with painkillers and muscle relaxants. My doctor says I have degenerative disc disease.

Santa Fe offers a grab bag of holistic healers, and I've tried a variety of treatments ranging from acupuncture to yoga, from diet therapy to psychotherapy. Today a new chiropractor straps me to his rack and makes some spinal adjustments so crunchingly loud that it sounds as if somebody just sat on a bag of tortilla chips.

I've tried to attack my relentless back pain with relaxation and meditation but so far with minimal results. My trial, though, makes me more sensitive to those whose pain is greater than my own. It forces me to be more attentive and reminds me that our physical gifts are limited and eventually wear out. Slowly, reluctantly, I am learning not so much to fight my pain as to accept it.

Why do we take ourselves so seriously? We are so afraid to make mistakes, have a good laugh and let our humanity show through. No matter how heavy our burden, there is always room to lighten up and put away our sensible shoes.

Humor is a notable gift in the game of Spiritual Pursuit. It is essential to forgiveness.

"I've got an amusing idea," said one of the old gods surveying the human comedy from high atop Mount Olympus. "As mortals grow older and less physically appealing, let's have their sex drives remain as strong as rutting goats."

"I love it!" cried Apollo.

"Done!" said Aphrodite.

Occasionally I get hurt and angry with others because I feel that they are not giving me my due of love or consideration. But the problem, I begin to see, lies not so much in their performance, but in my expectations. For me, it was a stunning revelation to realize that every person — without exception — is doing the very best that he or she can do.

Human love is highly selective, usually exclusive, often an extension of our own needy egos. It may encompass deals and trade-offs. Human love is always conditional and heavily laced with expectations; it tries to control.

The nature of God's grace, or spiritual love, is universal and non-selective, it sets no limits, draws no boundaries. It cannot be bought or sold. If we can open ourselves up to it, it flows through us.

When we bond with another person or another living being, we have already established a spiritual relationship based on mutual trust and a growing sense of completeness. A world soul makes its presence felt only when we extend the boundaries of our capacity to bond.

Although raising a child is not everyone's calling, what work could be more worthwhile? And who is better suited to raise your own child than you are? Why else would he or she be entrusted to your care? Regrettably this generation finds many parents delegating this sacred responsibility to strangers.

From where does this flaky notion come that says children need to be molded and pummeled into shape? That children are raw dough waiting for an adult to give them form and definition? Isn't it the adult who is fragmented, and the infant, fresh from God, who is complete? Can we recognize our children for the innate geniuses they are, and release them from the havoc inflicted by well-intentioned but misinformed adults?

If we want our children to value the world, we can take some bold and innovative steps to kick-start young imaginations. We might initiate a complete family media blackout — cancel magazines and newspapers. Pull the plug on radio and TV. Disconnect the phone. Stop all the cultural pollution flooding our homes and wasting our minds. How can we possibly hear the wind in the cottonwoods, or the crickets singing in the woodpile if our ears are always jammed with broadcast noise? How can we possibly hear each other? The tab we pay for our steady diet of junk food media is dear. It's time for a fast.

There are angels on the streets of Española. Albuquerque too! Angels abound but they're invisible to all but the very young and the very old. My brother Joe became childhood chums with a pair of cherubim called Aard and Seneca. In times past they had names like Jehoel, Melchisedec and Barbellato. Gabriel, Michael and Raphael, famed archangels, are currently on assignment in the former Soviet republics.

Today's winged messengers, guardians and guides prefer more contemporary names like Fred, Bep, Barbara and Doug. They continue, however, to cover us with their feathers and brush our lives in gentle and profound ways.

Happy is the man who knowingly walks with angels.

If I have a guardian angel, I'm most aware of it when I'm driving my Ram pickup. Admittedly I am not the world's best driver. Friends tell me never to chew gum *and* drive at the same time. Douglas even suggested that I give up driving altogether and give my truck to the Boys' Club! I take this chiding good-naturedly, but still, I wonder. In 35 years on the road, I've never had an accident. While I am the one behind the wheel, is someone else there, unseen, actually doing the navigating? And why? If there weren't someone to watch over me, would I have smacked into a tree long ago?

When Supreme Court Justice Potter Stewart was asked for a definition of pornography, he gave a memorable reply, "I know it when I see it." Grace, it seems, is equally difficult to put into words, but when it is there, we sense its warm and reassuring breath. We may even catch a glimpse of something nudging us toward sweet untrodden pastures.

On the first warm day of spring, I go up into the foothills of the Sangre de Cristo Mountains where the proud ponderosas grow. I lie down on the ground and listen as the wind blows through the long-needled pines. The ancient ones, the Anasazi, knew this same wistful sound. This same ceaseless whisper that is bringing stillness over me.

Ideas are like bees looking for the right flower to land on. If you want ideas to find you, be still and vulnerable as the meadow wildflowers and soon the bees will come.

Silence is the spring from which we draw our inner strength, the source of our assurance. Through thoughts and words and deeds we communicate with the rest of the world, but only through the quiet mind do we tabernacle with the Great Spirit.

Competition is manipulation. I want no part of it. Instead of comparing myself with others, I'd rather become transparent, stay out of my own way and allow the splendor which created me to shine through.

We never really discover anything; things are revealed to us.

God cannot operate where trust and secrecy are absent.

What's going on here, what is being described? How am I to interpret what is being described? For the first time, really, I'm reading The Bible. This is radical, revolutionary material! I am stunned by its strange collection of incredible tales, inspired by its radiant metaphors, dumbfounded by its supernatural encounters between man and spirit.

Since the early Christian movement began, the Scriptures have been constantly manipulated, revised and edited — yet they still continue to grab souls and transform lives. They *are* more fantastic than science fiction, more spellbinding than good mystery, more passionate than Gothic romance. Moreover, the King James Version remains a masterpiece of English literature. This indispensable companion and primer par excellence is here. This essential handbook on invisible activity.

When after many years, I read the Bible again on my own with no rigid theology to defend or personal motive to affirm, I merely brought to it a healthy curiosity and a flexible mind. How different this experience was from prior Sunday school readings or college studies. This time around no one told me what I believed or what doctrine to uphold or what dogma to adopt. I simply lost myself in the beauty of its text, transfixed by its marvelous power and the presence of holiness.

One of the most mystical and intriguing Biblical passages is found in The Gospel of Saint John: "All things were made by him; and without him was not any thing made that was made." Can this mean, I wonder, that God made all there is, and anything that God did not make was not made? That sin, death and disease (and anything else that God did not make) have no reality and have not been made — except in man's mind? Comprehending this idea can be powerful medicine for it blows to bits many of this world's most fundamental beliefs.

There must be a way for us as individuals to determine for ourselves whether or not a particular work authored by human hand is divinely inspired or not.

By becoming intimately acquainted with the material and living with it firsthand, we begin to get a personal sense of it. Does it ring true? Does it have a life of its own? Is it calculated to manipulate some people or does it offer universal truths which serve us all? Does it give Light?

The Bible is such a work, but not because tradition says so, or because scholars or clergy or anybody else says it is, but because it withstands all of our personal criteria. The high level of consciousness displayed in the Bible could not have been written by anyone lacking the most profound spiritual understanding. Consciousness of this magnitude is not of human origin.

Early this morning I take a long solitary hike in the high plains and watch cloud shadows roll slowly across the land toward the distant Ortiz and Sandia Mountains. I breathe in deeply the knife-sharp December air and snort the pungent scent of juniper and sage. There . . . the shrill cry of the noisy piñon jay! Suddenly I have crossed over. I am beyond time. The lone ranger has become the lone receiver. Mother Clay offers me her ageless love song.

3

CONVERSATIONS WITH RAVEN

*The animals
I sing for them.*

Teton Sioux

Man, that bright possibility, is the only species ever to inhabit Earth who is capable of contemplating his existence.

Daily I trot around the track at St. John's College. Often I am the only person there, but not the only intelligence. Frequently a large black raven flies over and lands on the grass nearby. First we watch each other. If there's no one else around, we talk.

In myths and fairy tales it is often animals or children who show the hero a way out of danger or difficulty. Native Americans have long recognized the healing magic of animals. Raven serves most willingly as my therapist and offers me steady encouragement.

In her deliberate and reliable contact with me, she eases my sense of alienation.

Like a fallen Dragonfly I was carried along with the current, powerless against the flow till something serendipitous occurred. Somewhere along the river's course, my soul sprang awake, realizing that what it had been living was a dream. A tiny flash of insight and the torrent's grip released. My battered wings were whole again, eager to hover and dart.

On the dingy streets of Istanbul I watch gypsies pull tame brown bears around by ropes attached to rings in their noses. As they yank the ropes, the bears stand on their hind legs and wave their front paws, "dancing" for the amusement of passers-by. Instantly I feel the pain of the steel ring in my nose and the utter humiliation of the bears. I cry for the mistreated, misunderstood beasts of this world.

Never fear. Whatever it takes to wake us up is just around the corner.

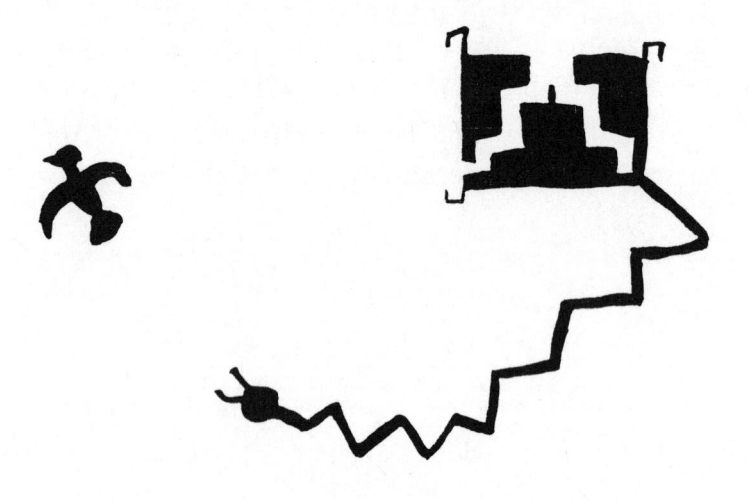

My mind is a menagerie crowded with imagined obligations. Rival interests clash within and vie for my attention — until I begin to distance myself from anything which contributes to my ongoing unconsciousness including individuals, institutions, activities, beliefs — anything which diverts me from my own exploration. Finding my own way is rewarding and exciting work but choices are difficult.

Jesus is most emphatic on this point and unusually tough. When a disciple presents him with a personal conflict of interests, Jesus replies, "Follow me; and let the dead bury their dead."

Anyone committed to metaphysical study inevitably begins to experience new alignments. As new interests develop, old interests begin to fade. Old friends and relations drop away; new friends and relationships are born. With the freedom to embrace new horizons, we may draw from a much larger pool — the human race — our true extended family.

Watch how Coyote Mother handles her quarrelsome pups. Study her ways. Notice how she detaches herself from their incessant chattering and petty squabbling. See how she keeps her own mouth shut.

I become increasingly aware the instant I put the judge away and start listening, when I open my eyes and ears to what there is around me. Strength and wisdom lie in observation, not criticism.

When you listen, you are one person. When you say something, you become another person.

"There's no such thing as *sin*," declared Puma after her long and arduous journey. "No such thing as Satan either. There is only ignorance, massive misperception and separation from Consciousness."

"Whew, that's a relief," said Jack Rabbit.

Which is more pathetic, today's hunter or the hunted? I grieve for the frightened eyes of animals under siege, but what of men whose endangered egos find consolation in the blood of our vanishing wildlife? We have been given dominion over the natural kingdom — not a license to destroy it. Our role is caretaker not executioner.

Flapjack nestles down on the sunny window sill. Patiently watching. Slowly blinking. Awaiting developments.

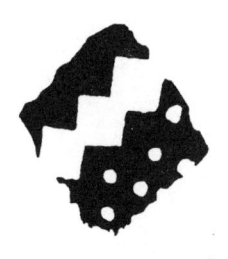

If only people would purr when they're pleased, hiss when they're pissed and not be so easily taken in by disguise. Cats are perfect.

As humans we come into this world kicking and screaming, mortal, vincible and sure to die a ghastly death. The question is: *Are* we human beings as the look of things suggest, or are we something else disguised as human beings as the prophets suggest?

I have learned a deep respect for Krishnamurti who writes:

"One cannot belong to any cult, to any group whatever if one is to come upon truth. The religious mind does not belong to any organization, to any group, to any sect; it has the quality of a global mind.

"A religious mind is a mind that is utterly free from all attachment, from all conclusions and concepts; it is dealing with what actually is; not with what should be."

It's 4 a.m. I'm wide awake. It's so quiet I can hear the cat gently snoring and the distant drone of a truck shifting gears. These unchartered hours just before dawn I call "the calling hours" when all is still and anything can happen. For me, this is the ideal time for mystical communication. Lines are open. Operators are waiting for your calls.

Nearly 30 years out of Hobart College and still, sometimes, I have nightmares about not being prepared for my final exams. Too many schools and universities encourage us to learn the hard way, out of fear of failure. This method has become so thoroughly established and so widely accepted, that we forget other more positive mechanisms which trigger our spontaneous urge to learn. How about some joy, some surprise, some delight?

Gary is discouraged. After months of looking for a worthwhile job, his search had turned up nothing. His pain was apparent. I wanted to help. We opened a bottle of Chianti Classico and talked over the kitchen table. After listening to his trials at some length, I suddenly burst out with, "If you want to do something meaningful, then why don't you stop looking and start listening?" I may be an occasional winebibber, but I have no advice to give. Trying to help a friend in need by offering personal advice is metaphysical malpractice. Answers to our inner dilemmas can only come from within.

Roadrunner searches for answers in every cult and crackpot religion he bumps into. When he's finally given up all faith and hope in finding any comfort there, he'll be closer than he's ever been.

Largemouth Frogs place a large and mindless value on celebrity and fame, whereas Smallmouth Frogs spend their summer afternoons in quiet anonymity — free to dip in their lustral pools in sublime peace and secrecy.

"The poetry does not matter," said T. S. Eliot. What the poet means, I think, is crucial to the success of our own self-discovery, that the results of our efforts — the poem, the painting, the pot — are not nearly as important as the process which brings them about. The real fulfillment in any personal expression lies not so much in the final product but in the process which brings it to life, for the process is constantly revealing.

Hazel is a teacher in the highest sense and unlike any teacher I've ever known before. She "teaches" me nothing. She simply encourages me to watch my own process. To see where I am coming from. To watch myself without judgment or evaluation. She alone understands that in the process lies the understanding. "Watch for signs of a mysterious happiness," she'd say. "Do anything that makes you happy. Drop your guilt. Be wherever you are."

Watching her at work in her classroom surrounded by stacks of her beloved books, I kept thinking to myself how impoverished the world is spiritually, and how we replace our spiritual hunger with our rapacious appetite for consumption and extravagance. Suddenly seized in a fit of admiration for my unlikely mentor, I looked at her and said, "Hazel, you have ruined me forever."

We are strongly attracted to vulnerability in children and adults. Is it their willingness to be open and unguarded which draws us in and makes us feel as if there is a place for us?

When you step outside yourself and begin to witness what you are doing, you become a spectator of yourself. You watch whatever it is that you do.

What is it about this place that makes people leave careers and commitments elsewhere and move here on little more than intuition or impulse? How deep is our need to be rooted in rich cultural soil. How compelling is the mystical connection we associate with present-day Pueblos, Navajos, Hopis, Apaches and Zũnis. How lonely we were on our high-rise terraces and suburban patios. How great is our need for community, simplicity, gentleness, tolerance and open sky!

Words are like keys to be fiddled with and examined. When selected carefully, they can unlock palaces; they can unlock rusty hearts. And like all valuable tools, they are not to be used indiscriminately.

These days there's a lot of attention paid to New Age pastimes such as channeling, past-life experience, crystal therapy, dolphin swims, rebirthing and so on. Soon these activities will be bumped by a host of new practices touted to expand our knowledge and self-awareness. There is nothing to lose by trying to keep the channels open, but what about "the channels"?

Myself, I want no intercessories, no middlemen. Only the most direct connection possible will do. Many New Age foibles focus on one aspect or another of the human condition or ego strengthening. "Will I find love?" "Will I be rich?" "Who was I in a past life?" Such questions may open worldly doors, they may amuse us, entertain us, even reassure us, but they have little to do with God's kingdom because their primary interest is the emphasis on *I*.

Think how differently our lives would be if
we stopped worrying about death. Lupe, my
full-figured cat, has no fear of death whatsoever,
but she does fret that she is not going to get chicken
bits for supper. Mostly she has peace.

When I follow my passion and refuse to compromise, I can accomplish astonishing feats I didn't know I was capable of. In answering my heart's desire, I am powerfully energized.

I long to bring forth that which is unique to me. To uncover, at least, a smidgen of the life puzzle. It seems that I have made scant headway in my quest, for the riddles are confounding and the labyrinth can be a lonely and forbidding place. I have lost my way many times and continue to do so. Still, with my daypack filled mostly with optimism, I keep pushing into unknown territory, willful to the end.

"Ever since Eden, you towering bipeds have been rotten to me and my kind," cries Snake. "You run over us on highways, taunt us with sticks, use our hides to decorate your silly handbags and cowboy boots! When are you going to stop your cars, get out and admire our graceful engineering as we glide across the road? Soon we, too, shall vanish from this earth."

Every living creature is a perfect model which we fail to see or understand. Every creative person is a constricted artery through which some faint pulse of creation throbs. Every newborn babe is an opportunity for peace which the world continues to ignore.

The whole *is* greater than the sum of its parts. In the full symphony of creation, no one plays alone. Every voice is welcomed.

It is man, not God, who has nailed mankind to the time/space cross, and in doing so has disconnected himself from the eternal Spirit. Jesus was sent here to demonstrate this message, but we wound up worshipping the messenger instead.

Exploitation is the long dark shadow of our spiritual bankruptcy. It kills everything it touches — integrity, art, intimacy, sex. The health of our fragile planet.

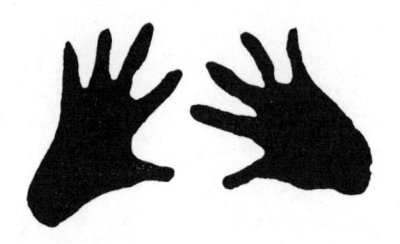

Alone at midnight out on the desert under the beckoning stars, I am completely disarmed and vulnerable. As my own fixed positions become distant, I begin to trust the silence and just be still. I ask of God sometimes that he lead me beside the still water that I might know his true reflection.

When I pray *for* something, I have misunderstood the nature of prayer. God does not run a mammoth convenience store where I can present my shopping list and stock up on needs in short supply. God knows perfectly well what my needs are, and in some inexplicable way these needs are met. But how could they necessarily jibe with the desires and expectations of one whose primary concern is self-preservation?

Meditation is remarkably like a thorough housecleaning. I sweep up all the accumulated fear, selfishness, rage, envy and whatever else builds up in dark corners and exhale it, slowly, out of my body through my breath.

When my place is relatively tidy and free of fetid thoughts, I breathe in the presence of love, of thanksgiving and forgiveness.

Then when all is washed and clean again, I invite the Great Mystery to come on in.

The teachings of Jesus are the clearest, most concise spiritual bequest that I know of. They embody essential information. Were we to understand his two great commandments perfectly, and live by them implicitly, we would make the quantum leap.

"Thou shalt love the Lord thy God with all thy heart, and with all thy soul, and with all thy mind.

"Thou shalt love thy neighbour as thyself."

Repetition is essential for understanding.
Repetition is essential for understanding.
Repetition is essential for understanding.

Let's totally re-invent Christmas or toss it on the scrap heap. The modern yuletide has become the most tiresome annual "should" of all. I'm not referring to the celebration of Christ's birth which Christmas is not. I'm describing the predictably dull, commercial, nerve-jingling frenzy which regularly grips Christendom every December. Christ would not be pleased at how we celebrate his birthday.

Jesus was born a human being much like the rest of us. By the time he was crucified a short 33 years later, he had already come into full possession of his divinity as Jesus The Christ. What happened to the lad during those intervening years? How was his transformation made? How did he unfold in wisdom, compassion and unrestricted love? How can we learn from his example? This is the message of the biblical Jesus; this is the message that we humans seem to miss continually.

4

TAPPING INTO THE MAGICAL

*Clearest, purest flint the heart
Living strong within me.*

Navajo

So as mortal beings we tread precariously, convinced of our progress, haunted by the specter of the past, driven by our endless fascination with getting and spending, taking little time, if any, to halt our daily grind long enough to discover who and what we really are.

There are continuous fields of flowers whose buds, for a bunch of reasons, remain tightly closed or sadly stunted. Those few buds which do manage to burst forth in fullest bloom we call "geniuses."

Never be ashamed to cry. There is much to cry about.

A rousing toast to all wanderers who find themselves disconnected from their source and from each other — those disenchanted, discouraged and dispirited. Those in dis-ease. Let us also salute the unmoved, unsung, unrealized parts of us, withering for lack of exercise. Here's to lost pieces!

We have been zapped by television. Seduced and abandoned by fashion and advertising. Pounded numb by the junk music of our age. Sucked dry by the addicted dysfunctional society which bred us, by the gross materialism of modern culture and the neurotic priorities we place on winning and commercial success.

We've been denied a meaningful education. We cannot read, cannot write, cannot express ourselves. We cannot see. We cannot hear. At no time in the history of humankind have so many souls been spiritually so betrayed by the cultural pollution in which they live.

All of us are damaged goods. Broken pots. Every reprobation, pain, barb, insult and indignity done to us has like repercussions. This and all the damage we in turn roll over to others is repairable, but unless we jolt ourselves from our perpetual sleepwalk, we merely continue the injury.

When my public success is measured in eyedroppers and failure is counted in crucibles, I try to remember that I learn as much from my failures as from my successes. Probably more.

I fear to surrender something I hold close, my ego. Change only comes about when Walter begins to let go of his self-importance.

My Career. My Success. My Family. My Self. My Religion. My Country. Food, Drugs, Sex or Alcohol. There are at least a dozen major gods in the modern pagan pantheon of dieties. Everybody has a god or two. We all put something first and foremost on our shopping list. At which altar do you pray?

They have told me who I am and what I can do. They have told me where I can go and what to expect when I get there. "Fiddle-deedee!" as Uncle Charlie Cooper used to say. None of it is so unless I choose to believe it is.

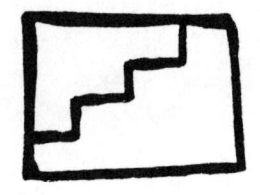

Either you stop smoking cigarettes or you don't. Either you stop abusing alcohol, drugs or eating too many calories or you don't. Huge organizations and industries have mushroomed, fostering the idea that you alone are incapable of quitting something harmful to you.

Nuts-pops! You — and only you — have the power to stop or start anything you deem necessary, including the abuse of addictive substances. They have no power over anybody — except the power we choose to give them. A bottle of drain cleaner can kill me quickly if I choose to drink it, but it has no power over me. I choose not to drink it.

The trouble with group activity is that those who tend to take control of such group programs often do it for purposes other than that for which the group was originally intended.

You think that you are an insignificant speck on a minor planet in an unimportant galaxy in the vast wilderness of space. In truth, you are the sole attention of God.

The very fact that you have been born is of the greatest significance.

"Nothing happens randomly in all creation," said Macaw. "There are no spare pieces in the Great Kiva — or the Mimbres Bowl. Every component has its place in the Universe. Every being has been given its own function as well. It's up to each of us to find out what that function is."

The gardener plants a tender young sprout which is starving for lack of nourishment. My job is to prepare fertile ground for it to grow. Tend the little shoot. Feed it. Soak it well with reverence. Protect it from the winterkill. Then stand back and behold a prodigy.

Our richest untapped natural resource is the wild child we hold inside, yet because of our fearful heart, we fail to set the rascal free. If we caught his capricious spirit and trusted his spontaneous whims, we would rely on him completely, for he's our long lost companion, our uninhibited guide.

Most of us just get by, tending our snug little dens and taking care of personal business. Others strive, often at considerable risk, for that piece of light just beyond their reach and for some purpose greater than their own. Those few individuals who lodge in our imagination and kindle inspiration always opt for the noble run.

Your spontaneous act of kindness blazes like a shooting star across the darkened meadows of heaven.

Every child, every tree, every porpoise, every pig and pup on the planet wants to connect with me if I can just lay down my hunting shield and wipe clean my war paint.

Can you tell just by looking at a person whether they are working from a state of grace? Not likely. God's agents prefer undercover operations. They are deft in the art of camouflage.

I am going to try a difficult experiment on you. I am going to love you unconditionally, without my usual checklist of requirements, and see what happens. Just in case.

A clutch of believers. A tangle of shoulds. A gang of gods. A gaggle of goddesses. A pride of egos. A herd of expectations. A shower of ideas. A spring of insights. A gusher of understandings. A river of revelations. A drove of devils. A parliament of judges. A coven of critics. A richness of laughter.

The world is weary of constipated old men who make the rules and wield their authority to impose their fearful dogma on others.

A small girl is said to have heard Christ's laughter as his soul was released from the cross.

Listen to your inner voice, be it faint as a bat squeak.

You are being summoned;
Surrender to the call.
If it don't happen *now*,
It don't happen at all!

If you realized that the nurtured spiritual part of yourself would accompany you on your eternal journey, and that everything else you have labored so hard to accumulate would vanish the instant you depart this world, would it alter your daily agenda?

Don't hesitate to tackle the bigger questions of your existence. To be inherently creative and exuberantly alive is to take on large perceptions of mortality, of God, of the meaning of life. We really have no idea of what our lives were meant to be or what our potential is. We were meant to probe and find out; to crawl, if we must, out of the drab cubicles of conventional thought. Great science and great art only come about through the struggle to break free from the familiar and the known.

Drop your cover story and face the truth about yourself. Trying to appear some way that you are not is self-defeating and exhausting. Others see through your charade anyway. Around 30, I suddenly ran out of excuses for not doing whatever it was my soul was hungry for. Slowly I began to trust me being me and cosmic tumblers began clicking into place. When I look back on it, I wonder why it took me so long to "come out." Being gay in a society which devalues of you is difficult at best, but being "queer" and not acknowledging it to yourself or those you care about is self-mutilation.

I needed to create for myself a nurturing environment. A place where I could live and work in an atmosphere of acceptance and support. I found such a place in Santa Fe, and the artist inside finally exploded like a ruptured piñata.

A painter also needs a space to fling paint, a place to try out his ideas in uninterrupted isolation. My studio became my living room, my sanctuary. It is where I make important discoveries about who and what I am.

Ron, an artist friend, recently joined a local health club and was changing in the locker room when a fellow member who had been playing golf casually asked, "What's your handicap?"

"Homosexual," replied Ron.

Escape from those who offer you easy answers to complex problems. From those who suggest that you need not assume responsibility for your life and its course. Psychics, mediums, fortune-tellers and astrologers are particularly suspect. Quackery and fakery mislead us into a false state of security.

Beware of evangelists, cultists, hucksters, healers and gurus whose hidden agenda is mental manipulation or financial control. Of those who trade on loneliness and credulity. The spiritual bandwagon is rife with charlatans and hokum.

In solitude and reverie we find our strength. Spirituality is a private affair.

If I live in Taos 40 years, I know Taos. I have a personal experience of Taos, not a belief in Taos. Knowing something and believing in something are two different animals. My desire is to know God, not to carry a belief in God.

In every age, in every culture, we all participate in creating our own reality. What we see out there before us is always a reflection of what is going on inside our collective consciousness. When you and I make meaningful inside changes, the world outside will change too.

When I want to know who Jesus was, I study his words and teachings directly from the Gospels. When I want to make acquaintance with Aquinas or Meister Eckhart, I read the writings of big thinkers. If the process of discovery ignites my imagination, then I find the actual journals of Thomas Edison, Albert Einstein or Marie Curie.

I cheat myself in delegating others to interpret for me, when I let reviewers, censors, biographers, editors, preachers and teachers tell me the meaning of things. I deprive myself of the thrill of my own discovery and rob myself of the magic of the firsthand experience. How quickly milk goes sour after it leaves the cow!

Despite the pervading myth of romantic love, happiness and fulfillment do not come to us from others. We extract them from ourselves. When I uncover a tiny sliver of joy, I want to keep on digging. Mother lodes lie buried below.

Everything starts and ends with you. Try approaching your life as if it were an epic poem, a masterful painting or a beautifully sculpted pot and give it all you've got.

Work without reason except for the love of the work itself, for that love may be trusted if not always understood. Give it your total commitment and the untamed years of your life before all zeal is squandered and all passions spent.

We can never teach anyone else how to love or how to see or how to become aware. Nor can we really tell anyone anything either — not in the highest sense. For each of us must discover essential information for himself. What we can do, however, is to honor our own integrity so that no one is disadvantaged by our enterprise.

Do you remember Eden? It occurs to me that some of us do. Adam and Eve were not its only tenants. Paradise is a part of every creature's experience, part of our genetic code; and some of us still remember fragments of the peaceable kingdom — whole and harmonious — where life was simple and humane. It may have been a garden glade or something else entirely. I can't quite recollect. It's just beyond the bonds of memory. Is it possible that when we have completed all that we were sent here to do, we might return to our Edenic state, rejoining lost affections?

My best efforts are those brief lines which employ few words and offer more to the imagination. We live in our imagination. I would like to connect with you without using any words at all, but along the towpath we've lost our native ability for telepathic and interspecies communication.

5

NEAR TO
THE PRIMAL HEART

*Preserving us along a safe road
May our roads be fulfilled.*

Zuñi

Does my work refresh me or exhaust me? Have I been coerced into doing it or was I naturally drawn to it? Does it absorb me or do I long to be doing something else? Do I wake in the morning excited to begin my day? Does what I do need doing? If the answers are *no*, then I have yet to make conscious union with my heart's desire.

"You've got to earn a living, son, become successful." And so it begins early on, the gentle shove away from one's own interest. The disapproval of following one's private destiny. In our ignorance, we believe we know what's best for our children. We want them to have every advantage, an edge on their peers, so we educate them to be competitive. Our idea of success becomes their idea of success, consequently the program that nature has drawn up for them is ignored.

A happy child does not need to be told what to do. He already knows what his interests are and where he wants to be. All a parent can do is love the child, respect his integrity and provide the nurturing environment in which to thrive in.

Once we find our center, everything else unfolds like frost crystals fanning out on frozen windowpanes. When I am centered and working from that place, I'm out of stress.

Oh, Santa Fe! When I first saw you 20 years ago, you were a dusty little town, difficult to get to, impossible to leave. An ancient village of desperados and dreamers hiding out in the mountains of northern New Mexico. An odd oasis of nonconformity. But soon your unique charms were discovered by those who recognized your commercial possibilities, and your simple adobe complexion was prettied up and packaged for the world.

Today you are all about style and tourism. Your innocence is mostly a memory, but there are still traces of it stashed behind garden walls and mesquite doors for those who care to look. And the landscape which surrounds you is still unbearably lovely and largely intact. The skies that cover you are still intensely blue and laced with cumulus clouds. Your air remains crystalline and fragrantly scented with piñon smoke and lilacs.

Moving to Santa Fe was like throwing open dozens of French doors in my heretofore tightly shuttered house.

Brilliant days and chilly nights. The late summer air has the look and flavor of crisp Chablis. Butter yellow aspen trees shimmer against ultramarine skies. Drifts of wildflowers blanket dirt roads and arid arroyos. Stands of purple sticky asters and cascades of saffron-colored chamisa. Spiky minarets of woolly mulleins and branchy prairie sunflowers. Long green tendrils of creeping buffalo gourds. Little golden zinnias and droopy Mexican hats. Clumps of crimson firewheel and choruses of deathly white datura trumpets. Autumn's richly embroidered opera cape has encircled my high desert home.

In my travels I have visited many fine pagodas, stupas, mosques, temples, cathedrals, basilicas, churches and the like, but I find I am easily distracted by the architecture and the art, the costumes and rituals, the strange smells and human activities which transpire there. I feel much closer to the source of things when I'm hoicking weeds from the garden or walking along the Pecos River.

I support myself as an artist, yet I feel more and more detached from the "artwork" displayed in local galleries. Southwest kitsch and mundane landscapes predominate. With some notable exceptions, the bulk of these creations is commerce, not art, and much of it simply trendy tourist trash, or art as bland accessory for interior decor. Art for dentists' offices! Its apparent success is painful to behold.

The function of art, for me, is to alter perceptions of how we see. Not always to comfort, confirm and pacify, but to provoke, challenge and reveal.

The most important artists working today are not artists in the traditional sense at all, but a potent handful of song writers, movie makers and rock musicians whose global vision, combined with their mastery of electronic media, allows them universal expression and appeal.

Art alone has the ability to linger on throughout the ages. Storytelling, music, dance, literature, photography, the decorative arts — they all have a life of their own. They nourish the world.

What we bring to the act of observation determines what we see. Each student in art class looks at the same model or still life and sees it differently. The most interesting artists see something not seen before.

Bleached bones, undulating hills, sensuous oversized flowers. The powerful paintings of Georgia O'Keeffe. But for me, her most indelible images are the many haunting photographs which exist of the artist herself. Always the solitary figure against a stark New Mexico landscape. One tumbleweed holding firm against the wind. O'Keeffe was totally committed to herself and her work. To her lifelong love affair with nature. I am fascinated by her singleminded view of the world, her moral grit. But mostly I am attracted by her fierce individuality. Her life and her work are solidly fused. What a sturdy presence she was.

It helps to have a sense of humor about art, but then it helps to have a sense of humor about anything if you're any good at it and particularly if you're not.

Writing, like painting, is an act of receiving. A communion of sorts. I don't know where it comes from.

Santa Fe is a jagged mosaic made up mostly of Hispanics, Anglos and Indians living together in tolerant coexistence. The vigorous art business takes full advantage of this curious ethnology by focusing on numerous exhibitions of "Indian Art," "Western Art," "Hispanic Art," "Contemporary Art," "Women's Art" and so on. Art or craft, folk art or "high art," the debates range on. It's difficult to understand those who are forever dividing up art and artists into tidy little categories. I see only art and non-art, artists and non-artists. What difference does it make what labels we place on those who make art? Art's a cross-dresser. Let's affirm the wonderful diversity of multicultural, non-sexist art. Talent knows no pigeonholes.

I have stopped painting for a while. I'm not sure why. How else can I pay the gas bill? I relish the act of putting paint to canvas, but not the nagging prospect of selling and promotion. Of painting for the likes of gallery owners and the art establishment. I'm sick of buying into this gross materialism which consumes the art world. Of putting out one more thing in this world to buy. I'm tired of being even a minuscule part of it. Today's art market is more interested in money-making and self-aggrandizement than it is with exploring the real possibilities inherent in the creative process. Art can be a powerful force in our transcendence, otherwise it just clutters up the place.

Along with the painted pots of early Native American culture, I am inspired by another legacy left behind by prehistoric peoples of the Rio Grande Valley. On the rock faces of canyon walls, lava escarpments and basalt boulders, I have discovered amiable constellations of strange images called *petroglyphs* carefully chipped in the hard stone by hand.

These rock art images reveal a cosmic circus of flute players, kachinas, plumed serpents, animals, shamans, starbeings, masks, shields, tracks and bizarre clan symbols whose meanings have been lost forever. It is with gratitude and deep respect that I draw on their mysterious meanings and powerful spirits to illustrate my own scratchings.

From a petroglyph pecked in stone a millennium ago by an Anasazi boy, to present-day graffiti sprayed on a subway car by an inner city youth, there's a timeless, irresistible urge to mark our territory with the epitaph, "I was here!"

Rock art has my rapt attention, as do the early artists who created it. Each secluded site was carefully chosen to face the warming sun, a conscious blend of nature, spirit, man, art. One senses that these "primitives" lived and breathed their spirit line, their spiritual connection.

I like it here. I like being with my glyphic friends and their enigmatic engravings. Here I feel a kinship. No need to make translations or interpret what I see. Just to be in this enchanted gallery surrounded by their ancient logos. To put my hand in their handprint and feel the primal pulse.

Creativity, it seems, is best expressed by those whose vision is unrestricted and unencumbered by the visible, the tangible, the solid concrete appearance of matter. By those who sense the elusive "otherness" of everyday human experience.

On the subject of sexuality, all I know is this. We have no more choice over our sexual orientation than we have over our skin tone or our eye color. Around puberty, we usually develop sexual feelings toward the opposite sex or toward those of our own sex. Either way, there need be no shame involved. The great diversity to be found in the erotic garden of the senses is clearly part of the plan. Unless we express our sexuality fully and without fear, whatever stripe it happens to be, we deny our own healthy functioning and self-esteem.

I long for a relationship of the deepest intimacy but mostly in fantasy. Should a likely candidate express interest, the old critic inside resurfaces, dredging up worn-out excuses why it could never work.

Perhaps, Stray Cat, you have spent too much of yourself pursuing Eros. Still, you have learned as much about life from the company of strangers as from the safety of friends.

I've never been attracted to those without just a little sin in their lives. A pinch of sin is like a dash of chile in the stew. Without it, life can taste duller than Wonder Bread. As we become conscious receivers of inner grace, we tend to leave the bulk of our "sins" behind and turn our attention to other matters, but I shall always catch and return the knowing glance in a hungry eye.

Profligate, moderate, celibate — and much to my astonishment, all three have offered merriment!

I've never known for sure if sharing a life with someone else is a free choice for each of us or not. It appears so, but many people (and artists in particular) seem to be more productive and happier by themselves. While there are times when I desperately miss the long-term companionship of a loving partner, I have also avoided the horrendous compromises which often accompany such relationships.

When I am strongly attracted to someone, I literally endow them with the most remarkable qualities and charms. On some occasions, I have been able to catch this amended beauty in a photographic portrait or a figure study. When the burner's off and I'm out of love, I look at them again and wonder what the fuss was all about.

Enter love's enchanting twisted maze, ye who dare.

Loving you takes nothing important from me. It enhances me.

Surrender is always voluntary. Should I demand your surrender, I only succeed in snuffing out that which I love.

Love demands of me and reveals as it unfolds. The most amazing revelations about myself have come about through my clumsy efforts to love you.

When we love one another humanly, we experience all of love's pleasures and all of its corresponding pains. Love's contradictions are continually laid out for us side by side. When we look to people for love, we may find it and we may not. When we look to God for love, we find it. What we are famished for are intimate relationships with God and with each other.

The toll road to my enlightenment is paved with paradox. Many of the insights and revelations one encounters along the way appear to contradict each other completely. Am I really Spirit made of godly stuff, I wonder, or just a frightened slab of temporary flesh hopelessly shackled in time and space? Am I following a selfless path of self-denial or am I just utterly selfish? Can I be holy *and* horny at the same time? My answers surely must be all of these. We are one of two. And both halves must be reckoned with; both must be exercised. Particularly the half we do not favor.

Working with Hazel is always tremendous fun because she recognizes the meaning and importance of play. Students in her design class are asked to build geometric models out of colored toothpicks and challenged to uncover the "underlying structure" of such puzzling intricacies as Moorish tile patterns, snowflakes and "the golden mean."

"Design is everything!" she says. "The way you set a table. The way you arrange color. The way you construct a tetrahedron. Through participatory design one learns principles, the eternal dance of relationships. Play is the spirit of finding out. That is really all there is."

Play is passion.
Passion is play.
Why did I put my
Playthings away?

Hard work and passion are two different trails although each can look like the other. Culturally we've been conditioned to believe in hard work. It doesn't matter so much what we do, we're told, as long as we prosper. Hard work comes out of the "shoulds," and we can easily become addicted to it. Sometimes we're sent to career consultants or guidance counselors so they can tell us where our aptitudes lie.

Passion comes from another place — from deep inside. No one can tell us where our passions lie, for they bubble up out of pure interest, curiosity and firsthand experience. Passion is not motivated by financial reward or any other sociological incentive. We never retire from our passion — unless we happen to be a ballerina or an airline pilot. From our earliest glimmerings onward, we need encouragement to offer ourselves to our passion, no matter how disappointing or odd it might appear to others.

As a boy growing up in central New York, I had a bulletin board in my room which I delighted in decorating according to the seasons as I had seen my teachers do in school. With scissors, I would carefully cut familiar shapes out of colored paper, arranging them agreeably on my cork board. Red and yellow oak leaves in autumn, snowflakes ushered in winter and pastel eggs meant spring.

When I look at my graphic hard-edge paintings of today, I note a similar process in their creation. The subject matter differs substantially, but the process of placing shapes and colors next to each other until just the right relationship is achieved remains my distinguishing motif. The joists of adulthood are the saplings of our youth.

Around 40, all issues of any significance, including passion, became spiritual in nature. At 50, I find I am developing something of an exit consciousness. Age has its insults, but each age also has its own joys and passions.

Jesus, too, seems to have chosen an unconventional lifestyle and his titanic legacy transformed the world forever. Why then are we so intolerant of those who choose to live their lives differently from us? It can be of no small significance that Jesus lived and worked outside the mainstream of his time. Nowhere in the Gospels, for example, do we find Mary or Joseph admonishing their boy, "Jesus, find yourself a nice Jewish girl, settle down, get married, raise a family."

Once we forget about earning a living and embrace fully the passion planted in us with all our trust and all our might, our needs are inexplicably met. By taking a giant leap of faith we somehow trigger the flow of supply. Many of us waste our lives trying to accumulate supply, but supply cannot be accumulated. It must be delivered daily, fresh, like good bread.

When we encounter someone who is deeply in touch with himself, and thereby with his spirituality, it is very exciting and tremendously contagious.

Any work which truly expresses God's manifold love is valid and needs to be done. Especially that work which no one else is doing.

When we find our *work*, everything else falls into place. We have something to offer the world and something to offer each other.

If there is a demon haunting my house, it is my own ego inviting me to believe that it is I who am responsible for my trivial success.

Sometimes my search for understanding becomes unbearably lonely. I feel utterly abandoned in my adobe, which I share with my two tabbies. True, I wanted a contemplative life with plenty of time and freedom to explore my solitary interests. And now that I've got it, I wonder what the hell it was for?

A track meet is on TV! With just a flick of the remote, I can catch all the company and excitement of competition. How easy it is to fall for it all over again, to surrender the wanting soul to the seductive blue light of a cathode-ray tube.

No, not today. Other voices beckon. Dim but persistent voices which I cannot as yet identify. They call for my attention and pique my curiosity. Mostly they summon the longings of an undeveloped heart. I pour the cats some kibble from the sack and look out the kitchen windows at the mountains.

When my work is heart-invested, I sleep well at night and look forward to each new day. My relationships run more smoothly. But what amazes me the most is the unexplained assistance I receive from sources which elude me.

Simple-minded poppycock or divinely provided truth? Overcooked or rashly underdone? Too much paprika, not enough dill? In deciphering the secret codes of self, I find that all the great reversals have come to roost in me. The alternating current of the heart is fragile as old roses and tough as cypress root.

6

HUNTING THE INHERITANCE

*O our Mother the Earth,
O our Father the Sky!*
                Tewa Pueblo

Did I choose to come here? Do I choose my departure time? Is my earth-span optional? All I'm certain of is this: I am here to cherish, not to conquer.

Once I focus attention on this stupendous human experiment of which I am a part and become a conscious participant, a crucial first step has been taken.

Despite welcoming loving parents and a supportive family, despite my ample American upbringing and the fact that until now anyway, I have escaped poverty, war and catastrophic illness, despite my relative good fortune on this earthly plane, I've always known I am a stranger here.

Nothing out there is certain. Even the stars scurry about when nobody's looking.

The same substances which make up celestial bodies also make up our physical bodies. We are built of star dust. Then *KERBANG!* Out of the whirlwind we are whisked away — our borrowed elements returned to earth or sea or sky. That short stretch of time we call our life is a blink of Owl's eye.

Dying may prove a stampede of panic, but death itself is nothing to fear. Right from the first bell, we knew we were going to die. We all die to this world. There is no pain after death, just as there was no pain before we were born. The burning question is, do we want to come back or do we want to move on?

Over a blue corn enchilada Forrest remarked, "Sleep and death are lessons in letting go. Sleep allows us to let go of the day, and death allows us to let go of the pain, the fear, the attachment to the human condition."

I am always amazed at how many of us are unable, or unwilling, to approach the subject of death. Death is the launching pad toward which we are all rapidly converging.

We want to know what happens to us after death. We want assurance, reassurance, life insurance! Deeply felt assurance, the kind which dissolves fear and gives us confidence, does not come to us from any book or any religion or any person. And it certainly is not conveyed through the pat answers of blind faith.

It only comes about through the personal experience.

You, who have difficulty accepting the possibility of an afterlife, consider this: Life itself is such a weird and miraculous business to begin with, that the same intelligence which brings us life might easily renew our subscription once our expiration date arrives.

Real history is a personal realization — the minute we thought of something which changed our life.

Once consciousness has unfolded, it may not be refolded.

Coincidence is an inadequate explanation for meaningful synchronicity. *Luck* is a stalwart young man knocking on your door. *Catastrophe* is an opportunity for growth.

Let's stand shoulder to shoulder witnessing together these cataclysmic changes just commencing right *behind* our eyes.

When you step back from what you are doing and look for the largest pattern you can find, you find an even larger pattern which encompasses it. We are forever getting snarled in the details, losing sight of the wider, more comprehensive picture.

I see humanity as a sprawling river-sea of which you and I are individual waves. We tend to think of ourselves as separate from the restless tide and distant from each other. If only we could realize that the secret of this thundering sea is that we are each minute but indispensable parts.

Early on, we were all highly perceptive beings with acute powers of observation and insight. We saw both the physical and spiritual realms with a fresh and accurate eye. We were innocent and vulnerable, playful and vital. We knew how to love and we knew how to trust. We held a light brush. We were children.

God shines brightest in the small curiosities.

Be merciful with my trees, my farmlands, my rivers, my seas. Be merciful with my animals. Be gentle with every man, every woman and every child who comes your way. Be gentle with yourself, for you are all part of the same Spirit. And far more a part of each other than you ever imagined possible.

— *Mother Clay*

It is our responsibility for whatever happens to ourselves and our ravaged planet. If we cared for our Earth Mother the same way we care for an abused child, we might reassume the terrestial stewardship which sustained and ennobled our ancestors. At this critical crossroads, the direction we choose shall determine our fate. Either we take careful inventory of the contents of our consciousness or we continue the perilous slide into the sinkhole of indifference and despair. The opportunity is here. Our choice is what we do with it.

When I began reading J. Buckminster Fuller, I had difficulty with his vocabulary. His ideas were unfathomable, his maps unnavigable. I was determined, however, to stick with it and little by little understanding began to seep in. Today I still have trouble understanding Fuller, but he has changed forever the way I perceive myself in relationship to the universe and to our own *Spaceship Earth*.

When Bucky was young and in despair, he once considered suicide. Finally he came to the conclusion: "You do not have the right to eliminate yourself, you do not belong to you. You belong to the universe. The significance of you will forever remain obscure to you, but you may assume that you are fulfilling your significance if you apply yourself to converting all your experience to the highest advantage of others."

Teachers, shamans and guides appear to us in unexpected wrappings. Peek inside the package.

In the crowded ark of mystical writers, my absolute favorite is Joel Goldsmith. Born in New York City in 1892, Goldsmith is a modern American mystic who exhibits with breath-taking clarity and insight the consciousness of Christ himself. In a world desperate for spiritual life, it seems odd that his magnificent books and tapes are little known.

"When you begin to realize that evil, as such, has been a part of your existence only through ignorance, and goodness has been a part of your existence only by the grace of God, you come to that place where you become an absolute instrument for the grace of God to flow. You become a blessing, not only to yourself, but to everyone who comes within range of your experience."

Give me the eyes to see those whose gaze is unable to connect with mine.

Rain is impersonal; it nourishes every rice paddy and wheat field. Stars, too, are nonselective and the sun never discriminates. Even the peach trees bear luscious peaches for us, whether we deserve them or not. God is never selective. He neither rewards nor punishes his creation.

Despite what nonsense we've been fed, there is no favored race or religion, no favored nation, sex or individual. We are all impersonal in the eyes of God.

If you can recognize yourself as whole and complete, despite massive material evidence to the contrary, then you are nobody's fool and well on your way to healing yourself and the planet.

What sets the mystic apart from the garden-variety seeker of truth? What secret fuel propels his "lift-off" from the visible and obvious into the ineffable and unseen? What spark ignites that sudden flame which transfigures a mere believer into one who intuitively *knows?* All of the world's luminous saints and prophets have come to the basic realization that Jesus did: "I and *my* Father are one."

A nadir of nurturings. A flight of fears. A siege of experts. A litter of litanies. A deceit of religions. A shoal of doubts. A plague of patriots. An abundance of difficulties. A pod of ponderings. A peep of integrity. A labor of loves. A triumph of truths.
A singular of God.

Through misuse and abuse (not to mention blanket exploitation), the word "God" has become a travesty for many. It's lost its juice! How does one employ a word which too often conjures up tired images of a crafty old geezer propped up in "heaven" pulling wise (but inscrutable) earthly strings, while knowing full well that the activity of God is anything but? The popular image is no match for the vital and creative force which suffuses the whole of life.

I like to think of God as more of an actioning verb than a stationary noun — as a loving, flowing, supplying, sustaining, unfolding activity.

Finding one's own source is always at odds with the compulsive need to adopt a rigid set of beliefs.

Bread for the journey is there for all to break — unless, ironically enough, you are a "true believer," a zealot or a religious fanatic.

Somewhere among the far-flung bits of pottery lies the whole bowl.

No matter how meager or how magnificent it may be, everyone has a state of consciousness. What seems in short supply is an enlightened state of God-consciousness.

Whatever state of mind I offer the world comes back to me in spades.

Jesus and other mystics were able to recognize and employ spiritual principles which enabled them to give sight to the blind, heal the sick, feed the hungry and perform all manner of life-affirming miracles. Can anyone who gains insight into these very same spiritual resources perform similar demonstrations?

Answers to difficult questions are available to us, but they lie in a comprehensive understanding of spiritual principles — not on the slippery turn of popular opinion.

Hazel is the only person I've ever known who is devoted to spiritual principles. She delights in their capacity to reveal mysteries. Once I asked her if she would make a list of these principles for the class to study and she declined, saying it was necessary for each one of us to discover them for ourselves.

"Catch a cosmic fish!" she'd say. "Get familiar with a principle. Offer yourself to it. Trust it. Let the principle become active in your life. Give it the acid test. See if it works or not. When the realization comes, you'll say to yourself, 'But I didn't do this!' Well, if you didn't do it, who did?"

Most of us who ride this exquisite blue-green opal we call *Earth* live in physical and spiritual poverty. We believe in *two* powers. The power of good and the power of evil. As long as we continue to believe in these two powers, we will be subject to both and victims of both. We remain lockstepped in our futile struggles against gargantuan odds. The waste in human lives and potential is staggering.

Evil exists only in the mind that believes in it.

The part of me that is of "this world" always wants to improve personal and global conditions. To patch things up! To remake myself and the human condition into a more peaceful, more harmonious state of being.

The part of me that is not of "this world" calls out for a thorough investigation.

"Should we give up the world altogether, forget all its problems?" interrupted Horned Toad.

"Of course not," snapped the Old Lizard, "but if we hold the Great Spirit in our hearts, the outer aspects of our lives take care of themselves."

"I don't believe it," said Horned Toad.

"I know," sighed the Old Lizard.

Recognizing the illusory nature of sin, disease, even death — indeed all forms of human discord and discontent — is to recognize the Omnipotence, Omniscience and Omnipresence of God. If God is "all-power," "all-knowledge" and "all-presence" as the three O's attest, then how can there possibly be God *and* something else? Evil in all of its disguises must then be a non-power, a nothingness.

Transcending the infinite sorrows and limitations imposed on me by this mass belief in two powers thus becomes my primary task. The restitution of God, as the only power there is, is my only purpose.

Now that I know it in my head, I need to find it in my heart.

Blemishes and all, a lost masterpiece is currently undergoing restoration and recovery. Marred by misperception and the devastation wrought by ignorance and fear, we are just beginning to see the original brilliance concealed deep beneath ancient layers of neglect. In our willingness to take time out and strip away the cumulate grime of centuries, we can again attend the freshly painted moment of God's spectacular masterwork and rejoin the gallery of the living.

Ultimately one welcomes a spiritual experience with a quiet inner recognition of the Presence, or we pass it by unnoticed in our haste.

You know I can't prove to you anything recorded here, but some keenly independent part of us all knows whether or not a shard is genuine.

"Well," said the Old Lizard, "do you realize who designed the web you spin?"

"I didn't when I started," replied the Spider. "But in the course of spinning, an unexpected peace came over me."

"Amen," said the Old Lizard.

ACKNOWLEDGMENTS

Special thanks are due my friends Jennifer Dewey, Nathaniel Messimer, Blythe Brennan, Kay Hatton and Elaine Bland who read the manuscript and made valuable suggestions. I am most grateful to Alicia Yerburgh and John Schiff who helped edit the rough manuscript, and especially to Sonja Kravanja who pulled the final manuscript together.

I wish to thank Lewis Nightingale, who found a typeface; Douglas Atwill for his perennial support and many contributions; and Douglas Bland, my partner, for his encouragement and patience. To Barbara Nichols and Marie Stilkind, my editors, whose enthusiasm for *SHARDS* never wavered. Finally I am devoted to Hazel Larsen Archer who honors that which is within me and *is* me.

CHAPTER NOTES

Chapter 1

Page

1   1. A. Grove Day, **The Sky Clears** (Lincoln: University of Nebraska Press, A Bison Book, 1964), p. 113.

40   2. "Gospel of John," chap. 18, ver. 36, **The Holy Bible**, King James Version.

Chapter 2

41   1. Day, **The Sky Clears**, p. 91.

52   2. "Gospel of Matthew," chap. 6, ver. 28, 30-33, **The Holy Bible**.

78   3. "Gospel of John," chap. 1, ver. 3, **The Holy Bible**.

Chapter 3

81   1. Day, **The Sky Clears**, p. 23.

87   2. "Gospel of Matthew," chap. 8, ver. 22, **The Holy Bible**.

95	3. J. Krishnamurti, **The Flame of Attention** (San Francisco: Harper & Row, 1983), p. 26.
100	4. T. S. Eliot, "East Coker," Part II, **The Complete Poems & Plays 1909-1950**, (New York: Harcourt, Brace & World, 1952), p. 125.
118	5. "Gospel of Matthew," chap. 22, ver. 37 & 39, **The Holy Bible**.

Chapter 4

121	1. Day, **The Sky Clears**, p. 92.

Chapter 5

161	1. Day, **The Sky Clears**, p. 74.

Chapter 6

201	1. Day, **The Sky Clears**, p. 76.
217	2. John Love, "Interview with Buckminster Fuller," *QUEST Magazine*, Nov.-Dec. 1979, vol. 3, no. 8, p. 104.
219	3. Joel S. Goldsmith, **Beyond Words And Thoughts**, (Secaucus, N.J.: The Citadel Press, 1968), p. 128.
223	4. "Gospel of John," chap. 10, ver. 30, **The Holy Bible**.

NURTURE YOUR BODY AND SOUL WITH Changes® MAGAZINE

The Nation's Leading Personal Growth Magazine!

CHANGES is the only national self-help magazine that keeps you informed about the latest and best in personal growth and recovery. It brings you valuable insights that will help bring healing and wholeness into the most significant areas in your life.

★ Relationships ★ Mental, physical and emotional wellness
★ Self-esteem ★ Spiritual growth

Each issue of CHANGES features the best, most inspirational writers and thinkers of our time — articles and interviews with authors like J. Keith Miller, John Bradshaw, Nathaniel Branden, Janet Woititz and others who give the gift of self-understanding to millions of people.

CHANGES brings you practical ways to apply the positive, life-affirming philosophy of recovery to family life and friendships, to schools and the workplace, to the changing world around us.

Let CHANGES help you make positive, effective changes to enhance *your* world. A one-year subscription is just $18* for six bi-monthly issues. Plus, you'll receive lots of valuable book, conference and local seminar information.

Subscribe today by mailing the coupon below, or call us toll-free:

1-800-441-5569

and give the operator this number: HBWC92

Clip this coupon and mail it to:
CHANGES Magazine, Subscriber Services, 3201 S.W. 15th Street, Deerfield Beach, FL 33442-8190.

☐ **YES**, enter my subscription to CHANGES for just $18*/year.

Name: _____
Address: _____
City: _____ State: _____ Zip: _____
HBWC92

☐ Payment enclosed ☐ Bill me   Charge my: ☐ VISA ☐ MC   Exp. Date: _____

Signature: _____   Card #: _____

Please allow 4-6 weeks for your first issue.
*Florida residents add 6% sales tax. For Canadian and Foreign orders, add $20 for postage.